CONTENTS

Scriptures are taken from the King James Version of the Bible. Because we are aware that some terminology in the KJV is difficult for beginning readers, several verses have been simplified.

The Standard Publishing Company, Cincinnati, Ohio
A division of Standex International Corporation

©1996 by
The Standard Publishing Company
All rights reserved
Printed in the United States
of America

03 02 01 00 99 98 97 96   5 4 3 2 1
ISBN #0-7847-0420-1

THIS WAY to FUN!

You've checked all your lists, and you're ready to go, right? Well, just in case you need more convincing that crafts really are important—check below! Then look at the clipboard on the next page!

CRAFTS TEACH :

★ responsibility for materials, tools, and cleanup
★ discipline of completing a project
★ independence in work skills
★ teamwork in sharing materials, tools, and space

CRAFTS DEVELOP :

★ creativity—there is no "right" way
★ confidence—"I did it myself"
★ enjoyment of simple, inexpensive activities
★ basic physical skills, using different muscle groups

CRAFTS BRING TO MIND :

★ church as a happy place
★ my teacher as a special person
★ a special Scripture verse or Bible story

★ ideas to worship God
★ the plan of salvation

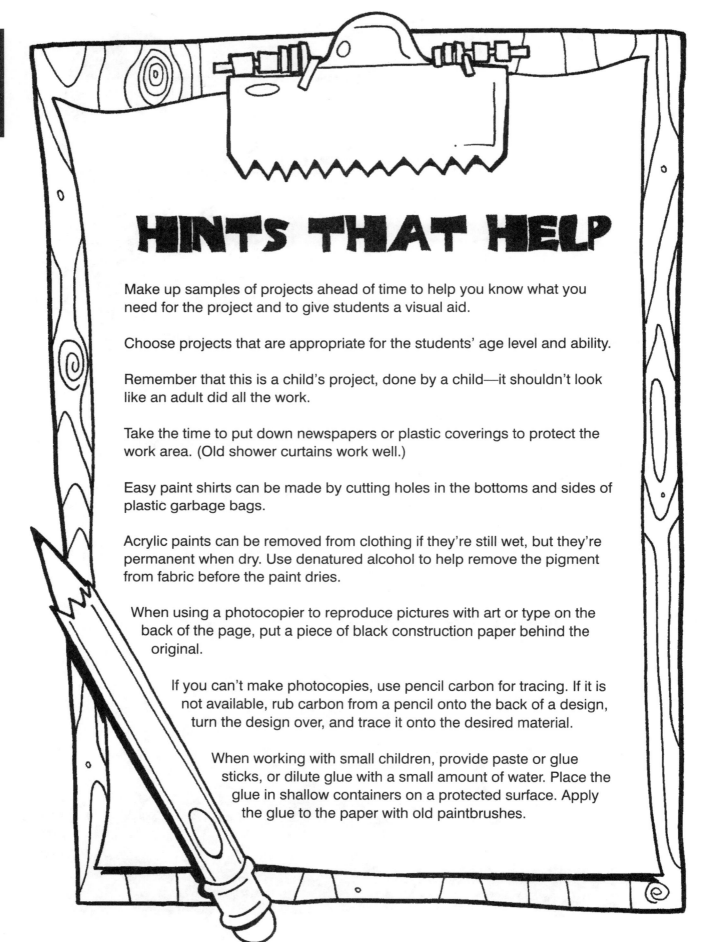

HINTS THAT HELP

Make up samples of projects ahead of time to help you know what you need for the project and to give students a visual aid.

Choose projects that are appropriate for the students' age level and ability.

Remember that this is a child's project, done by a child—it shouldn't look like an adult did all the work.

Take the time to put down newspapers or plastic coverings to protect the work area. (Old shower curtains work well.)

Easy paint shirts can be made by cutting holes in the bottoms and sides of plastic garbage bags.

Acrylic paints can be removed from clothing if they're still wet, but they're permanent when dry. Use denatured alcohol to help remove the pigment from fabric before the paint dries.

When using a photocopier to reproduce pictures with art or type on the back of the page, put a piece of black construction paper behind the original.

If you can't make photocopies, use pencil carbon for tracing. If it is not available, rub carbon from a pencil onto the back of a design, turn the design over, and trace it onto the desired material.

When working with small children, provide paste or glue sticks, or dilute glue with a small amount of water. Place the glue in shallow containers on a protected surface. Apply the glue to the paper with old paintbrushes.

PRESCHOOL/ KINDERGARTEN

PRESCHOOLERS

- ★ can't sit still for very long.
- ★ learn by doing and by repetition.
- ★ learn by touching, tasting, smelling, seeing, and hearing.
- ★ are learning to share, help, and take turns.
- ★ have not mastered scissors, coloring in lines, and folding on lines.

KINDERGARTNERS

- ★ like a variety of methods and materials.
- ★ can use scissors, glue, large crayons, and large paintbrushes.
- ★ enjoy laughing and giggling and may be mischievous.
- ★ like to ask "why?" and want to have reasons for what they are doing.
- ★ seek approval from adults for their behavior and their craft projects.

So THEREFORE...

Remember that the process is more important than the finished product.
Choose appropriate projects that the student (not the teacher) can finish.
Be prepared with coverings and cleanup materials—some messiness is inevitable.
Share the love of Jesus in your attitude, your voice, and your actions.

FOLLOW THE FOOTPRINTS AND LEARN THE BIBLE VERSE

Have children color the picture. Help them cut it out along the border.
Frame the picture by gluing it to a piece of colored construction paper.

©1996 by the Standard Publishing Company. Permission is granted to reproduce this page for educational and ministry use only—not for resale.

Wear and Share Visor

You will need:

- a copy of the pattern
- a piece of cardboard at least 6" x 10"
- a hole punch
- a piece of elastic 12" long
- tape
- crayons or markers for decorating

1. Copy the pattern. Mount it on a piece of cardboard and cut it out.

2. After the child has colored the visor, punch a hole in each tip, about ½" from the end.

3. Cut a piece of elastic about 12" long. Thread it through a hole, tie and reinforce with tape. Adjust to fit the child's head, then tie and reinforce the other end.

This **Wear and Share Visor** will help children let their friends know of their love for Jesus.

©1996 by the Standard Publishing Company. Permission is granted to reproduce this page for educational and ministry use only—not for resale.

Copy and color the picture, and glue it to construction paper.
Add sand, sea shells, and star stickers. Talk about following Jesus.

©1996 by the Standard Publishing Company. Permission is granted to reproduce this page for educational and ministry use only—not for resale.

Bee Kind Mini Poster

You will need:
- copies of the mini poster
- crayons or markers
- construction paper
- velcro dots or scraps of flannel

1. Color and cut out the mini poster and the bee, and mount the poster on a sheet of construction paper.
2. Place a velcro dot or a scrap of flannel on the bee, the hive, and the flower.
3. Move the bee back and forth as you talk about ways to be kind for Jesus.

 ©1996 by the Standard Publishing Company. Permission is granted to reproduce this page for educational and ministry use only—not for resale.

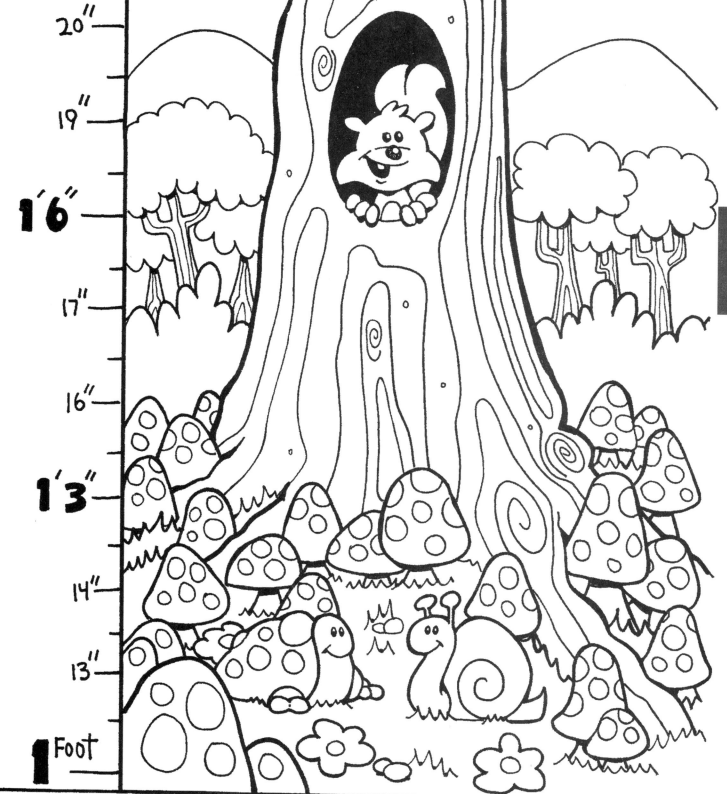

20"
19"
1'6"
17"
16"
1'3"
14"
13"
1 Foot

"Grow to Be Like Jesus" Tree

1. Copy four sections of artwork per child. (See the next three pages.)

2. Cut out all sections, and allow the children to color them as desired.

3. Assemble the pages with clear tape, as shown. Punch a hole in the top of the chart and attach yarn for a hanger.

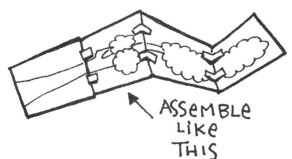

ASSEMBLE LIKE THIS

©1996 by the Standard Publishing Company. Permission is granted to reproduce this page for educational and ministry use only—not for resale.

11

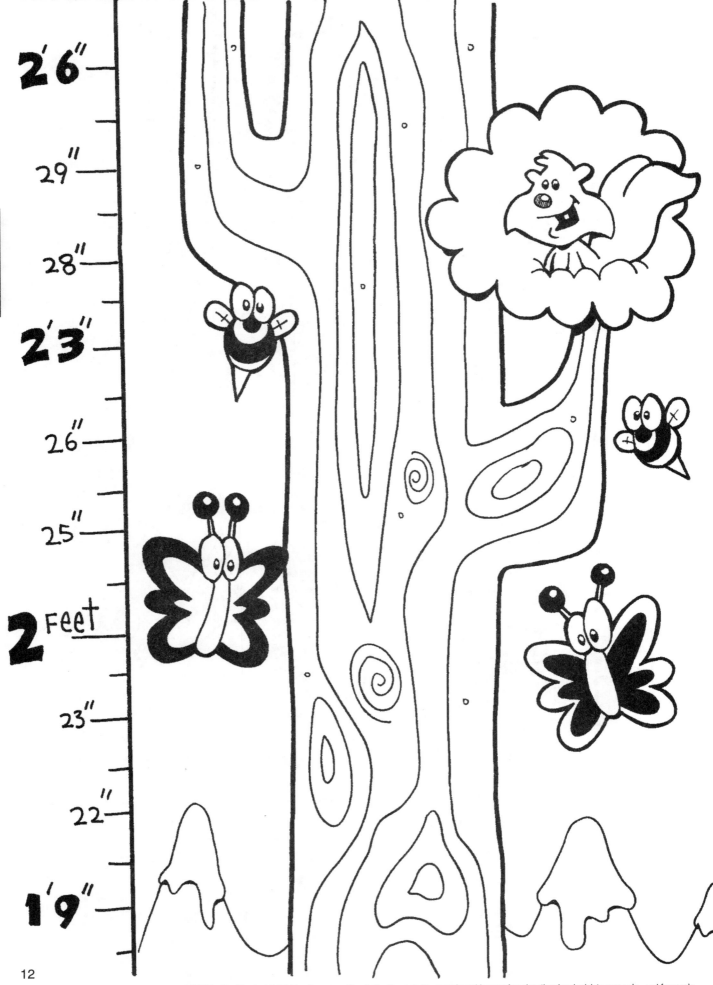

2'6"
29"
28"
2'3"
26"
25"
2 Feet
23"
22"
1'9"

Pre—Kind

12

©1996 by the Standard Publishing Company. Permission is granted to reproduce this page for educational and ministry use only—not for resale.

41"

40"

3' 3"

38"

37"

3 Feet

35"

34"

2' 9"

32

31"

©1996 by the Standard Publishing Company. Permission is granted to reproduce this page for educational and ministry use only—not for resale.

GROW TO BE LIKE JESUS

4' 3"

50"

49

4 Feet

47"

46"

3' 9"

44

43

3' 6"

Pre—Kind

©1996 by the Standard Publishing Company. Permission is granted to reproduce this page for educational and ministry use only—not for resale.

DESIGN A CAMPER

Reproduce the camper pattern and glue the pattern onto construction paper. Help the children cut out their campers and use crayons to decorate them. Glitter, rickrack or other trim, ribbons, and buttons may also be glued to the campers. See the next page for additional camper clothing. As the children decorate their campers, remind them to thank God—for taking care of them, for clothes, homes, and the world.

Pre—Kind

©1996 by the Standard Publishing Company. Permission is granted to reproduce this page for educational and ministry use only—not for resale.

CUPCaKe PRaise PaLs

You will need:
- paper cupcake holders
- light cardboard or construction paper
- crayons
- glue

1. Copy the faces and leaves on this page and the background artwork on the next page. Mount them on construction paper if you wish.

2. Have the children color the pieces as they like.

3. Glue the faces in the centers of four cupcake papers, then glue the leaves and cupcake papers to the background. Talk about all God has given us. Thank Him for His goodness.

GIVE THANKS

TO GOD

HE

IS GOOD

FROM PSALM 100:5

©1996 by the Standard Publishing Company. Permission is granted to reproduce this page for educational and ministry use only—not for resale.

©1996 by the Standard Publishing Company. Permission is granted to reproduce this page for educational and ministry use only—not for resale.

FUZZY FOLLOWER

Pre—Kind

You will need:
- four 6" paper plates
- paper fasteners
- glue
- pattern for head, hat, and feet
- flannel scraps or other fuzzy material

1. Have the children color the backs of the four paper plates. Attach the plates together, overlapping each plate and connecting with glue or paper fasteners.
2. Copy the feet, head, and hat, and have the children color them.
3. Glue flannel scraps or some other fuzzy material to the hat, and attach the hat to the head with glue or a paper fastener.
4. Attach two feet to each paper plate as shown using paper fasteners.

This Fuzzy Follower is a wonderful reminder that we should follow Jesus.

©1996 by the Standard Publishing Company. Permission is granted to reproduce this page for educational and ministry use only—not for resale.

©1996 by the Standard Publishing Company. Permission is granted to reproduce this page for educational and ministry use only—not for resale.

NEW CREATION MAGNET/MOBILE

Pre—Kind

You will need:
- 2 coffee filters
- food coloring
- one clothespin (not spring-type)
- chenille wire
- moveable eyes
- felt pens
- glue
- magents, or yarn (optional)

PIPE CLEANER

MOVABLE EYES →

CLOTHESPIN →

MAGNET

COFFEE FILTER →

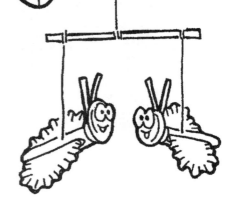

1. Wet two coffee filters and squeeze the water out. Place them flat on a paper towel.
2. Drop food coloring on the coffee filters, using any color or combinations of color. Allow the filters to dry.
3. Help the children color the clothespin with the felt pens, and create a face with the pens and moveable eyes.
4. Help the children wrap the chenille wire around the neck to make the antennae.
5. Push the dry coffee filters into the clothespin as shown and secure them with glue.
6. Add a magnet to the bottom of the clothespin; or, to make a mobile, slide yarn through the upper half of the clothespin and tie. Talk about how Jesus gives us new life, or about the beauty of God's creation.

©1996 by the Standard Publishing Company. Permission is granted to reproduce this page for educational and ministry use only—not for resale.

PRIMARY / MIDDLER

PRIMARIES

★ need to know they are loved and supported by the teacher, but enjoy the freedom of working independently.
★ are happiest when participating in a purposeful activity (in which they know the "hows" and "whys").
★ need honest praise, encouragement, and opportunities for success.
★ want challenging craft activities but have not yet developed fine-muscle coordination.

MIDDLERS

★ are developing physically at a steady but slow pace.
★ are curious explorers, and want to know "why" they are doing something.
★ want to be allowed to express themselves.
★ are searching for self-identity, but still respond to gentle guidance and encouragement from adults.

So Therefore...

Show a finished sample of the activity or project. Explain it thoroughly so students know the "whys" and "hows" for the project.

Give help as needed, but allow as much self-expression as possible.

Be prepared for some good-natured rowdiness.

Provide cleanup materials and have the students clean up on their own as much as possible.

Have other activities or projects planned for those who finish quickly. This helps to allay any possible discipline problems ahead of time.

PET ROCK PRAYER PAL

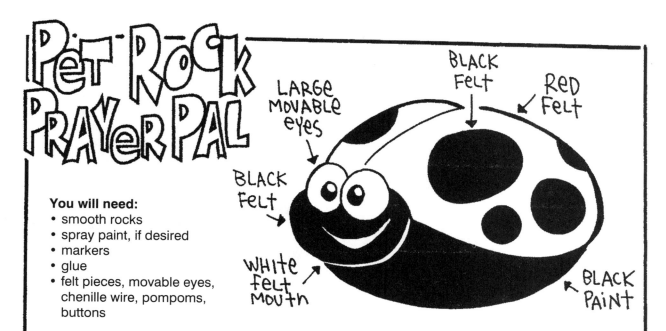

You will need:
- smooth rocks
- spray paint, if desired
- markers
- glue
- felt pieces, movable eyes, chenille wire, pompoms, buttons

Design an animal using felt, eyes, chenille wire, and trim. The rocks can be spray painted first, if you wish.

The pet rock will become a prayer pal to serve as a reminder of all God's gifts and tell us that any time is prayer time.

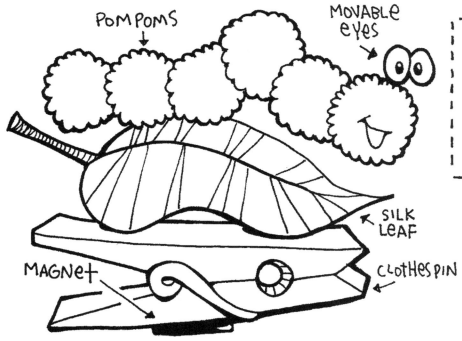

ALWAYS TRUST JESUS

Color a clothespin with a felt marker, or paint it with tempera. Glue on a silk leaf, pompoms, and magnet as shown. Add moveable eyes. Cut out the "always trust Jesus" note, or write a note of your own as a reminder of God's care.

NOTE HOLDER

©1996 by the Standard Publishing Company. Permission is granted to reproduce this page for educational and ministry use only—not for resale.

Pri—Mld

©1996 by the Standard Publishing Company. Permission is granted to reproduce this page for educational and ministry use only—not for resale.

JESUS LIFTS ME UP

©1996 by the Standard Publishing Company. Permission is granted to reproduce this page for educational and ministry use only—not for resale.

CREATE YOUR OWN THUMBPRINT POSTER

You will need:
- poster art on the following page
- an ink pad, or thin poster paint in a plastic lid

Copy the poster art on the following page, and let students create one-of-a-kind thumbprint posters.

Copy this page and let the children practice making thumbprint people and animals. First, have them make a row of thumbprints. Add features one at a time to make creatures as shown

thumbprint

dots and circles
for eyes
BIG smile!

two lines for arms
two lines for legs

add circles for
hands and feet

26   ©1996 by the Standard Publishing Company. Permission is granted to reproduce this page for educational and ministry use only—not for resale.

Pri—Mld

I AM SPECIAL
THIS I KNOW-

FOR MY THUMBPRINT TELLS
ME SO-

NO ONE ELSE HAS
ONE LIKE ME . . .

I'M AS SPECIAL AS CAN BE

BECAUSE JESUS LOVES ME
HE'S THINKING OF ME

HE MADE ME SPECIAL
HE MADE ME-
"ONE-OF-A" KIND !

PSALM 139:14

©1996 by the Standard Publishing Company. Permission is granted to reproduce this page for educational and ministry use only—not for resale.

MeMORY MOUSE

GOD'S WORD
WILL HIDE

IN MY HEART

FROM PSALM 119:11

You will need:
- 8½" x 11" plywood (¼"), or heavy board/foam core base.
- corrugated cardboard or foam core (⅛") for base
- 2" x 3½" fake fur or felt
- small pompom
- 36" cord or shoelace
- black felt marker
- glue
- jigsaw (for wood) or craft knife
- needle and thread

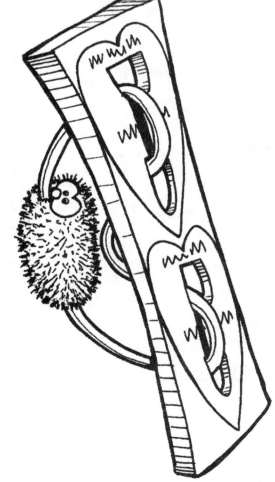

1. Copy the mouse house pattern onto the wood/card-board/foam core base.

2. Cut out the mouse house shapes. (If you are using wood, drill a hole in the shape before you begin working with the jigsaw.)

3. Sew the ends of the fake fur to one section of the cord. Form a rounded shape and stitch to form the mouse.

4. Add eyes with the felt pen and glue on the pompom for the nose.

5. Lace the cord through the mouse house holes. Sew the ends together to form a continuous loop.

6. Pull the cord and watch the mouse scurry through the mouse holes as you recite a Bible verse.

©1996 by the Standard Publishing Company. Permission is granted to reproduce this page for educational and ministry use only—not for resale.

FUN FRAME

1. Using the pattern below, draw pencil lines on a sheet of heavy cardboard. Cut on the lines to form the frame.
2. Cut out a backing sheet from poster board or a shirt box.
3. Cut small shapes from colorful summer shades of paper. Fold strips accordion-style and punch out circles.
4. Glue shapes to the frame.
5. Glue backing onto the frame along the two sides and the bottom.
6. Copy the picture of Jesus and insert it into the frame.

Option: decorate the frame with dried leaves and twigs.

FRONT

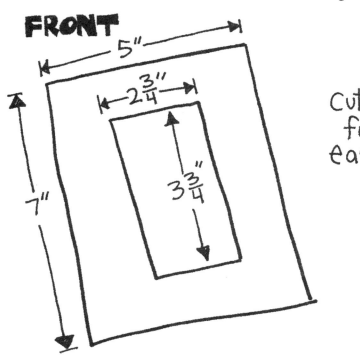

5"
2 3/4"
3 3/4"
7"

BACK

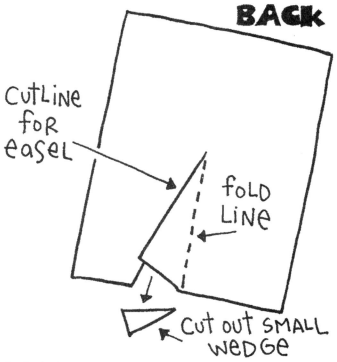

cutline for easel

fold line

cut out small wedge

©1996 by the Standard Publishing Company. Permission is granted to reproduce this page for educational and ministry use only—not for resale.

TiN CaN CAMPeR

1. Punch two holes in the bottom of each can as shown in sketch A.
2. Fold twine in half and tie a loop to make a handle (sketch B).
3. Insert the twine through the holes of the largest can and tie buttons, bells, or beads just inside the edge of the can. See sketch C.
4. Pull the twine up so the buttons are tight against the top of the can. Insert the twine through the holes of the next smaller can and repeat the tying instructions. Repeat for the smallest can.
5. Copy and color the face, hands, and shoes. Use tape to attach them as shown in sketch D.

Just as the camper grows tall, we can grow for Jesus. How can you grow as you serve Him?

You will need:
- 3 tin cans, graduated sizes
- 24" twine, cord, or heavy string
- 6 large beads, bells, or buttons
- tape
- juice can opener

 ©1996 by the Standard Publishing Company. Permission is granted to reproduce this page for educational and ministry use only—not for resale.

©1996 by the Standard Publishing Company. Permission is granted to reproduce this page for educational and ministry use only—not for resale.

WIGGLE PUPPET

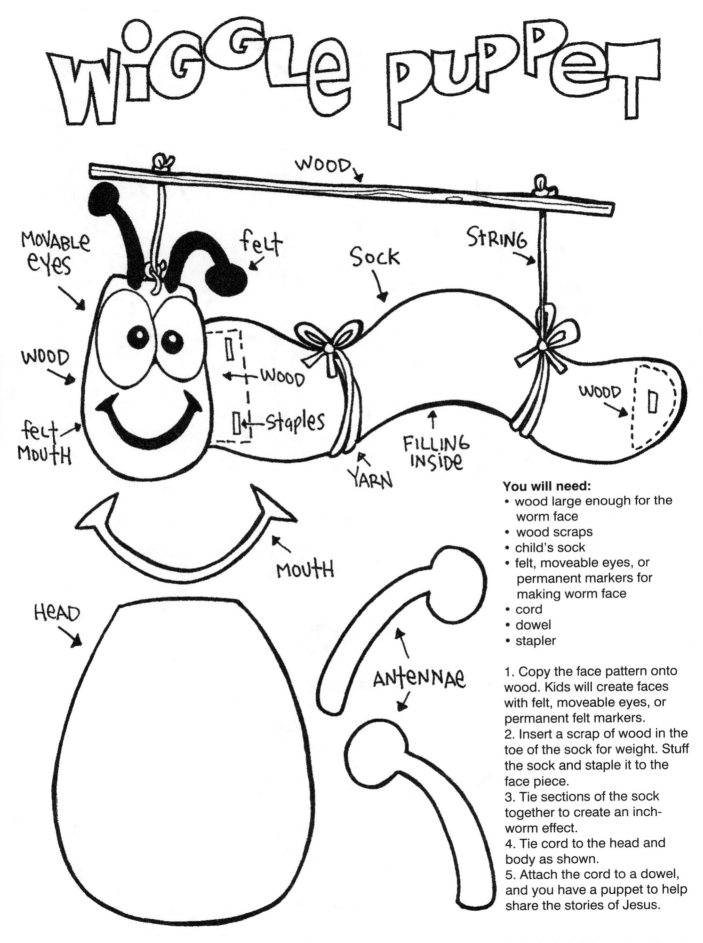

WOOD

MOVABLE EYES

felt

Sock

STRING

WOOD

felt MOUTH

WOOD

staples

YARN

FILLING INSIDE

WOOD

MOUTH

HEAD

ANTENNAE

You will need:
- wood large enough for the worm face
- wood scraps
- child's sock
- felt, moveable eyes, or permanent markers for making worm face
- cord
- dowel
- stapler

1. Copy the face pattern onto wood. Kids will create faces with felt, moveable eyes, or permanent felt markers.
2. Insert a scrap of wood in the toe of the sock for weight. Stuff the sock and staple it to the face piece.
3. Tie sections of the sock together to create an inch-worm effect.
4. Tie cord to the head and body as shown.
5. Attach the cord to a dowel, and you have a puppet to help share the stories of Jesus.

Pri—Mid

©1996 by the Standard Publishing Company. Permission is granted to reproduce this page for educational and ministry use only—not for resale.

BUNDLES OF BLESSINGS BEADS AND THINGS

Copy the triangle onto heavy posterboard and cut it out. Using it as a pattern, trace triangles from colorful magazine pages or church bulletin covers. Cut them out. Starting with the wide end of the triangle, wrap the paper shape tightly around a toothpick, and hold the end in place with glue. Slowly slide the bead off the toothpick. Coat beads with white glue and string them when dry. To make a placemat, enlarge the pattern and wrap on a 6" dowel.

SUPER STUFF "AUTOGRAPH PILLOW"

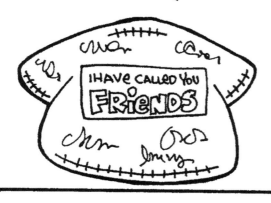

Copy the pattern or write the slogan below on the front of an infant-size T-shirt. Color the design with fabric pens. Turn the shirt inside out and glue or sew it together at the sleeves and bottom. Turn the shirt right side out and stuff it with fiber fill or similar stuffing. Sew the neck together and have friends sign their autographs. Use the pillow as a reminder of Jesus, the greatest friend.

I HAVE CALLED YOU FRIENDS

JOHN 15:15

©1996 by the Standard Publishing Company. Permission is granted to reproduce this page for educational and ministry use only—not for resale.

BEAN BAG TOSS

You will need:
- plywood (17" x 24"), 2 blocks 3" high
- 6 soup cans
- hot glue gun
- markers
- bean bags or balls
- tape

1. Peel labels from clean tin cans. Tape around the top to cover the rough edges.
2. Copy and color the camp critters. Cut out and glue them around the cans.
3. Place 3" blocks under one end of the plywood.
4. Attach the blocks to the plywood with a glue gun (ADULTS ONLY), and attach the cans to the plywood as shown.
5. Designate a value to each can and play a toss game for points. Or place quiz questions in each can, and answer the question where the ball or bean bag lands.

 ©1996 by the Standard Publishing Company. Permission is granted to reproduce this page for educational and ministry use only—not for resale.

BUG BITES

You will need:
- a piece of wood
- spring-type clothespins
- felt pens or colored pencils
- glue
- cord or yarn for hanging

Copy the critters and glue them to heavy cardboard. Cut them out and glue them to clothespins. Attach the clothespins to the wood so they open at the bottom, as shown in the sketch. Add a hanger of yarn or cord. Clip encouraging notes to family members, or special Bible verses, with the clothespins. Hang the note holder in a prominent place.

Pri—Mid

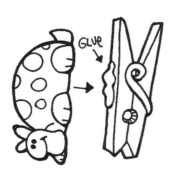

©1996 by the Standard Publishing Company. Permission is granted to reproduce this page for educational and ministry use only—not for resale.

RUBBeR STAMPS

You will need:

1. Copy the shapes and trace them onto sheet rubber, a foam meat tray, or craft foam. Carefully cut out the shapes.

2. Place a shape on one block of wood, and glue it into place using white glue. Allow it to dry thoroughly.

3. Ink shape stamps on an ink pad, and stamp shapes on paper. Use the stamps to decorate cards, posters, placemats, or signs.

Create a camp card to encourage a friend.

©1996 by the Standard Publishing Company. Permission is granted to reproduce this page for educational and ministry use only—not for resale.

Pri—Mld

FLY BY BUDDY

You will need:
- scissors
- glue
- crayons or felt pens
- a plastic straw

1. Copy the pattern.
2. Color the bird. Fold the pattern at the center and cut it out.
3. Glue the sides and top of the bird together, but DO NOT glue the bottom edge.
4. Insert a straw in the opening at the bottom of the bird. Point the bird upward and blow through the straw.

©1996 by the Standard Publishing Company. Permission is granted to reproduce this page for educational and ministry use only—not for resale.

SUN CATCHER MOBILE

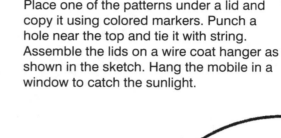

You will need:
- clear round plastic lids from deli containers
- patterns
- permanent markers
- hole punch
- string

Place one of the patterns under a lid and copy it using colored markers. Punch a hole near the top and tie it with string. Assemble the lids on a wire coat hanger as shown in the sketch. Hang the mobile in a window to catch the sunlight.

THEY THAT WAIT UPON THE LORD SHALL

MOUNT UP WITH WINGS AS EAGLES...

WALK AND NOT FAINT
ISAIAH 40:31

RUN AND NOT GROW WEARY...

©1996 by the Standard Publishing Company. Permission is granted to reproduce this page for educational and ministry use only—not for resale.

5TH - 6TH / TEEN

5TH - 6TH

★ Are beginning their growth spurts, and consequently will suffer mood swings.
★ Love competition, but often lack confidence in their abilities.
★ Are strongly motivated by peer pressure, and are looking for heroes to imitate.
★ Appreciate some attention, but are uncomfortable with outwardly emotional displays of affection or attention.

YOUNG TEENS

★ Are growing rapidly and becoming more sexually aware.
★ Are developing their own self concepts, and need to be accepted for who they are.
★ Put up fronts sometimes, and can be outwardly cruel to each other.
★ Need significant Christian adult examples who are not afraid to confront them if needed.

So THEREFORE...

Remember to provide appropriate projects that will sufficiently challenge students, but will be fun too.

Remember to plan adequately—for the project itself, and for those students who finish quickly.

Provide opportunities for fellowship and sharing together during the craft time for bonding among the students themselves and among students and teachers.

Be an example of Christian love—because it may be a real challenge! Don't take everything a young teen says literally. But don't be afraid to confront or talk with students; they can spot a counterfeit a mile away.

WeARABLe ART

Camp Shirt/Nature "T"

1. Lay shirt flat on a hard surface.
2. Place plain paper under the front of the shirt, so that colors will not bleed through.
3. Position leaves of varying sizes and colors on the front of the shirt to create the desired effect. Tape them in place.
4. Cover the design with plain paper or a paper bag.
5. Transfer the color onto the shirt by pounding the area covering the design with a rock. Check the results, and repeat if necessary.
6. Remove the tape and leaves from the shirt. Outline the design with fabric pens and paint as desired.

You will need:
• solid color T-shirts
• fabric paints or spray paint
• tape
• straight pins
• paper or plastic for covering work area

Turn to page 43 for more T-shirt instructions.

5th/6th—Teen

©1996 by the Standard Publishing Company. Permission is granted to reproduce this page for educational and ministry use only—not for resale.

©1996 by the Standard Publishing Company. Permission is granted to reproduce this page for educational and ministry use only—not for resale.

LET US RUN WITH PATIENCE

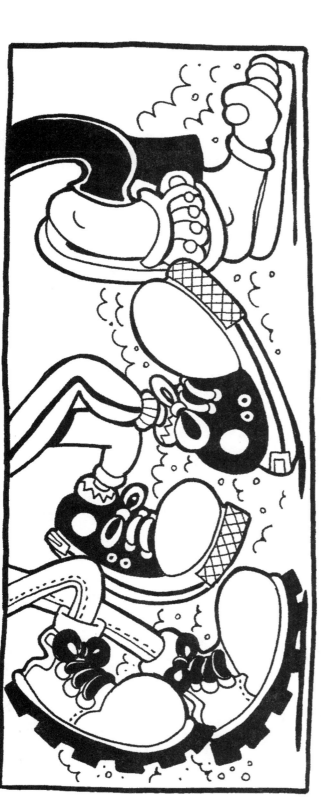

THE RACE THAT IS SET BEFORE US

HeBReWS 12:1

5th/6th—Teen

Run the Race "T"

Place this pattern under the front of a light-colored T-shirt. Trace the design with a pencil. Then remove the pattern and finish the design with fabric paints or fabric markers.

Spray Paint "T"

1. Copy the "Follow Jesus" pattern from the previous page. Cut out the letters and feet in order to form a stencil.
2. Place the stencil on the shirt and secure it with straight pins.
3. Place the T-shirt on newspapers. Insert a sheet of cardboard into the shirt so the paint will not bleed through.
4. Spray paint the shirt and allow to dry.

©1996 by the Standard Publishing Company. Permission is granted to reproduce this page for educational and ministry use only—not for resale.

BUILDING A
GUITAR BIRDHOUSE

① COPY THE GUITAR PATTERN (ENLARGE TO 7" WIDE × 9" HIGH) ON TO TWO ¼" PIECES OF WOOD THEN CUT THEM OUT...

② CUT A 1" HOLE IN THE TOP GUITAR PIECE

③ DRAW ANY DESIGN YOU WANT ONTO TOP PIECE AND PAINT WITH ACRYLIC PAINT (BE SURE TO ALLOW FOR THE ARM TO BE POSITIONED AT THE TOP)

④ CUT 44 RECTANGULAR PIECES ½" × 3¼" × ¼"

⑤ USING WOOD GLUE (F-26 ADHESIVE WORKS WELL) ATTACH 1½" × 3¼" PIECES TO THE BOTTOM PIECE OF THE GUITAR

⑥ NOW GLUE THE TOP IN PLACE

⑦ USE THE PATTERN TO CUT OUT ARM

⑧ GLUE ARM TO THE TOP AND INSERT THE ¼" × 2" DOWEL INTO A ¼" HOLE AND SECURE WITH GLUE

⑨ INSERT SCREW EYES IN THE WOOD THEN TIE WITH HEAVY FISHING LINE OR CHAIN

5th/6th—Teen

©1996 by the Standard Publishing Company. Permission is granted to reproduce this page for educational and ministry use only—not for resale.

Guitar Birdhouse

ENLARGE 120%

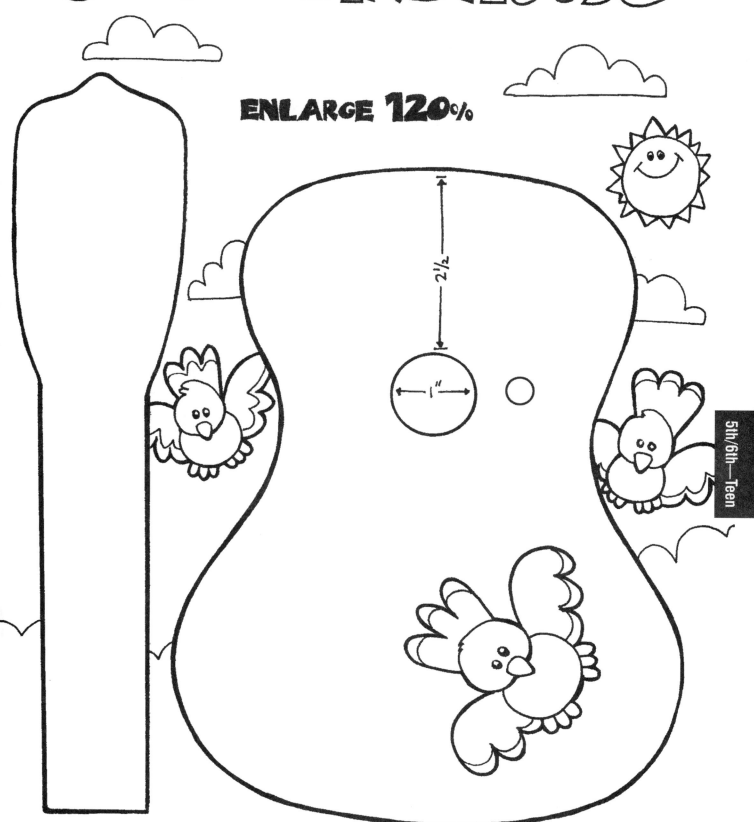

2½

1"

5th/6th—Teen

©1996 by the Standard Publishing Company. Permission is granted to reproduce this page for educational and ministry use only—not for resale.

Tin Can Lantern
CREATE A MOBILE

Choose one of the patterns on the next page and tape it to the outside of a clean tin can. Place a log inside the can. Put a nail (point down) on one of the dots in the pattern. Hit the nail once with a hammer to punch a small hole in the can. Repeat, moving around the design to complete it. Don't punch the holes too close together. Also, make two holes near the top rim of the can to use for the handle. Remove the log and the pattern.

Cut an X in the center of the bottom of the can. From the outside, push the edges up inside the can to hold the candle. Don't put your hand inside the can, if you can avoid it, because the rim and the edges of the holes you punched are sharp. Thread wire through the holes to make the handle, and place a candle in the bottom. Use the same nail-punch process on frozen juice can lids to make a mobile. Attach them to a wire coat hanger as shown.

46   ©1996 by the Standard Publishing Company. Permission is granted to reproduce this page for educational and ministry use only—not for resale.

©1996 by the Standard Publishing Company. Permission is granted to reproduce this page for educational and ministry use only—not for resale.

FLOWER FLATTENER

©1996 by the Standard Publishing Company. Permission is granted to reproduce this page for educational and ministry use only—not for resale.

5th/6th—Teen

GLUE to CARD

WING NUT →

TOP BOARD →

NEWSPAPER

FLOWERS/ Leaves

Bottom BOARD

You will need:
- two sheets of plywood, ¼-½" thick
- four 3" screws
- four wing nuts
- fresh flowers (small ones, not too thick, will give the best results)
- newspapers

1. Copy the pattern on the previous page onto a ¼-½" thick piece of wood for the top of the press.

2. Cut another piece of wood identical in shape for the bottom. It will not need a design.

3. Align the two pieces of wood and drill four ¼" holes as shown.

4. Insert four 3" screws from the bottom.

5. Position flowers on several layers of newspaper. Cover them with additional sheets of newspaper.

6. Use wing nuts to tighten the press. Allow several days for the flowers to dry. Remove them carefully, and glue them to a heavy sheet of white paper to make a greeting card.

©1996 by the Standard Publishing Company. Permission is granted to reproduce this page for educational and ministry use only—not for resale.

IT'S COOL TO FOLLOW JESUS

Copy the patterns. Glue them to cardboard or heavy paper. Color them and cut them out. Punch a hole in the top and add a tassel.

Play a Game Card

Copy and color the card pattern on the following page. Color the checkerboard grid as desired. Fold on the dotted lines to make a card, and write a note to a friend. Put the card in an envelope with small buttons or beans for checkers. Deliver the note and visit while you play.

©1996 by the Standard Publishing Company. Permission is granted to reproduce this page for educational and ministry use only—not for resale.

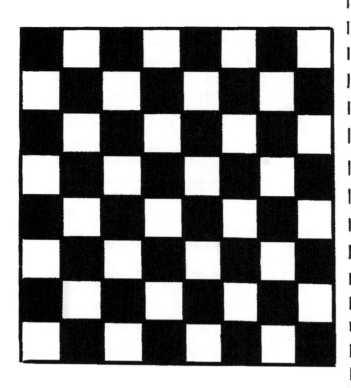

- - - FOLD - - - - - - - - -

FROM!

TO.

FOLD

5th/6th—Teen

TO.

FROM

IN EVERTHING GIVE THANKS;
FOR THIS IS THE WILL OF GOD...
1THESSALONIANS 5:8

ORIGINAL DESIGN BY:

©1996 by the Standard Publishing Company. Permission is granted to reproduce this page for educational and ministry use only—not for resale.

JESUS LIGHTS MY WAY

You will need:
- small jar or clear bottle
- 2½" piece of candle wick
- candle wax or paraffin
- double boiler
- colored sand, or salt and chalk mixture

1. Copy the animals below, or create your own design. Cut out the art and place it inside a small clear bottle so it faces out.
2. Trace the design onto the outside of the jar using a permanent felt-tipped marker. Remove the pattern from the jar.
3. Using boiling water, soften a plastic spoon and bend the handle up to create a scoop. Carefully spoon colored sand or colored salt* into the bottle. Make several colorful layers, and leave about 1½" at the top of the jar empty.
4. Melt candle wax or paraffin in a double boiler (NOT a microwave). DO NOT do this without adult supervision. Carefully pour the liquid wax into the jar over the sand. Fill the jar almost to the top. Place a wick in the center of the jar, leaving an inch or so sticking out.

* To make colored salt, dump some salt on newsprint. Rub it vigorously with brightly-colored chalk, and collect both the salt and chalk dust in a container.

5th/6th—Teen

©1996 by the Standard Publishing Company. Permission is granted to reproduce this page for educational and ministry use only—not for resale.

SUN COOKER

You will need:
- a 3-ounce paper cup
- one apple slice
- a sheet of black construction paper
- a small sheet of white poster board (8½" x 11")
- plastic wrap
- masking tape
- a rubber band
- a sheet of aluminum foil large enough to cover the poster board

1. Cut the black construction paper so it fits inside the cup. Then put the apple slice in, and arrange the plastic wrap over the cup. Secure with the rubber band.
2. Cover the poster board with aluminum foil.
3. Wrap the foil-covered board around the cup so that it looks like a cone with the foil side in. Tape the cone around the cup, and arrange it so it will stand up in the sun. Surrounding it with rocks works well.
4. Leave the cooker for a few hours, then check to see if you have a cooked apple! Warmer temperatures allow the apple to cook faster.

5th/6th—Teen

©1996 by the Standard Publishing Company. Permission is granted to reproduce this page for educational and ministry use only—not for resale.

CLOTHES MOOSE

Picking up clothes and belongings isn't such a chore when you have an "a-moose-ing" rack to hang them on!

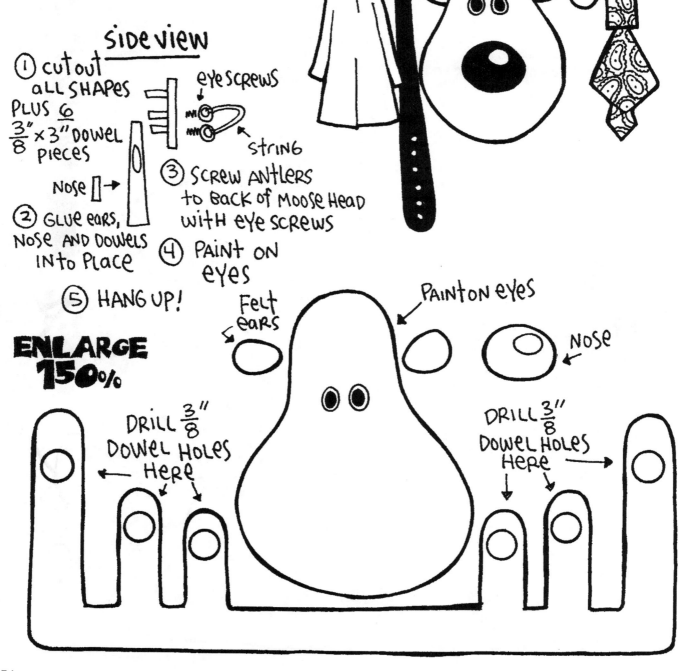

side view

① cut out all SHAPES PLUS 6 $\frac{3}{8}$" × 3" DOWEL PIECES

NOSE ▯ →

② GLUE ears, NOSE AND DOWELS INTO PLACE

eye screws

string

③ SCREW ANTLERS to BACK OF MOOSE HEAD WITH EYE SCREWS

④ PAINT ON EYES

⑤ HANG UP!

ENLARGE 150%

Felt ears

PAINT ON eyes

NOSE

DRILL $\frac{3}{8}$" DOWEL HOLES HERE

DRILL $\frac{3}{8}$" DOWEL HOLES HERE

5th/6th—Teen

©1996 by the Standard Publishing Company. Permission is granted to reproduce this page for educational and ministry use only—not for resale.

TIN CAN ICE CREAM

1. Mix milk, cream, sugar, vanilla, fruit, and nuts in the 1-pound coffee can. Seal with the plastic lid, and if necessary, put wide waterproof tape around the lid rim to prevent leakage.

2. Place the 1-pound can inside the 3-pound can and pack around it with layered ice and salt. Seal the 3-pound can with its lid.

3. Roll the cans back and forth briskly on the sidewalk or on a table for ten minutes. Open the cans and stir the ice cream with a spatula.

4. Empty the salt and ice mixture, and return the smaller can to the larger. Pack with ice only, and leave until ready to serve. Yields six ½-cup servings.

You will need:
- an empty, clean, 1-pound coffee can with lid
- an empty, clean 3-pound coffee can with lid
- ¾ cup rock salt
- ice nuggets
- 1 cup milk
- 1 cup whipping cream
- ½ cup sugar
- ½ teaspoon vanilla
- nuts and fruit as desired

FROZEN BANANA ON A STICK

Melt chocolate chips in a microwave or double boiler. Peel a banana. Insert a popsicle stick into one end and dip the banana into the chocolate. Roll in chopped nuts or sprinkles. Wrap the banana in foil and freeze.

GELATIN CATERPILLAR

Mix two family-size boxes of lime gelatin with 2½ cups boiling liquid (1 cup apple juice, 1½ cups water). Stir until dissolved, then pour into rounded ice-cube trays. Refrigerate until set, several hours or overnight. Remove the gelatin forms by placing the tray in hot water for a few minutes, then using a knife to loosen them. Create a body by placing each piece of gelatin on pretzel sticks. Form a face with icing, trims, or licorice.

Food-n-Fun

©1996 by the Standard Publishing Company. Permission is granted to reproduce this page for educational and ministry use only—not for resale.

MORE SMORES

Combine graham crackers, toasted marshmallows, and chocolate bars—or substitute peanut butter cups or peppermint patties for the chocolate.

Mix ⅔ parts ginger ale, ⅓ part club soda, and 8-10 raisins in a glass. Watch the raisins jump around!

Combine cranberry juice, lemon-lime carbonated drink, and sherbet. Make ice cubes from the lemon-lime drink, with a cherry in the center of each.

BUG JUICE

LADYBUG TREAT

Use one scoop of strawberry ice cream and one small scoop of chocolate ice cream for the body and head of the lady bug. Use chocolate chips for spots and eyes, licorice for antennae, and icing for the mouth.

CAMP SANDWICH

Get a 6-foot loaf of bread from a bakery, sliced in half lengthwise. Fill with meat, cheese, lettuce and tomato, or whatever you like. Lay the sandwich across giant pretzel sticks or apple slices (for legs). Use cauliflower for ears, olives for eyes. Coat the top of the sandwich with a thin glaze of honey and add sunflower or poppy seeds.

Food–n–Fun

©1996 by the Standard Publishing Company. Permission is granted to reproduce this page for educational and ministry use only—not for resale.

You will need:
- a piece of wood slightly larger than your artwork
- felt pens
- glue
- fine sandpaper
- clear shellac

1. Enlarge and copy the sign. Color with felt pens.
2. Glue to a piece of wood and allow to dry.
3. Coat the wood with shellac and allow to dry.
4. Lightly sand the surface and apply another coat of shellac.
5. Sand again, shellac again, and add a hanger to the back.

SOME JOYFUL SOUNDS

You will need:
- 5 bolts of various sizes
- one dowel, 8½" long
- 2 beads to fit over the ends of the dowel
- yarn or cord

Assemble as shown in the sketch. Be sure the bolts are close together to produce sound, and hang freely.

You'll be nuts with delight over the sound of bolts.

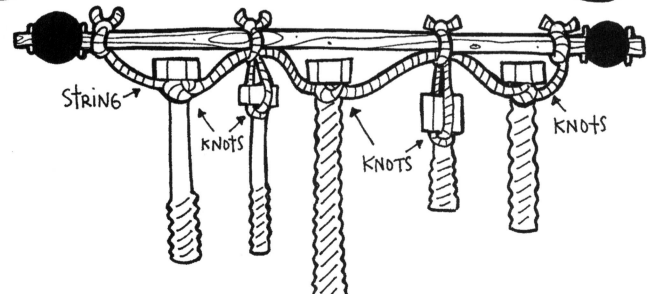

STRING → KNOTS KNOTS KNOTS

Food—n—Fun

©1996 by the Standard Publishing Company. Permission is granted to reproduce this page for educational and ministry use only—not for resale.

DRUMS

You will need:
- empty can or cookie tin
- clear food wrap or large balloon
- heavy rubber bands
- materials for decorating (paper, markers, scissors)
- dowel pieces
- bead or styrofoam ball
- paint
- felt

To make a large drum:

1. Remove the lid from a large empty potato chip or popcorn can. Stretch a double thickness of cellophane wrap* over the top of the can and secure it with a heavy rubber band. Stretch the clear wrap tight.

2. Measure a large sheet of paper to fit within ½" of the top and bottom of the can. Lay it out flat and design and color as desired. Use the art on the next page if you wish. Attach the design to the can with tape.

3. Make a drum stick, if you like. Paint a dowel. Glue a plastic or wooden bead to the end, and allow to dry thoroughly.

To make a small drum:

1. Cut the bottom from a cookie tin. With the lid on the top, stretch a double thickness of cellophane wrap* over the bottom of the tin, and secure it in place with a large rubber band. Invert the can, remove the lid, and put wrap over the top so the can has wrap on both ends.

2. Measure paper to within ½" of the top and bottom of the can. Lay it out flat and color or design as desired. Attach the design to the can with tape.

3. To make a drum stick, decorate a dowel with paint or colored tape. Glue a styrofoam ball to the stick. Cover the ball with a piece of colorful felt and tie it with yarn.

*Instead of clear wrap, you may use a large balloon cut and stretched over the opening.

©1996 by the Standard Publishing Company. Permission is granted to reproduce this page for educational and ministry use only—not for resale.

©1996 by the Standard Publishing Company. Permission is granted to reproduce this page for educational and ministry use only—not for resale.

Food-n-Fun

GUIRO

pronounced GWEER-oh

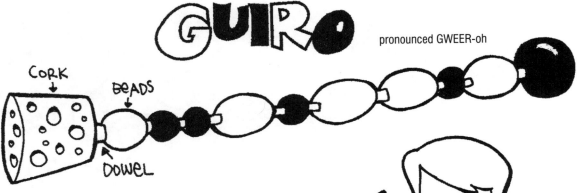

You will need:
- a cork
- wire coat hanger
- beads of various sizes
- paint
- wire cutter
- wood dowel

1. Cut a wire coat hanger to about 15" long. Push the cork onto one end and glue it into place.
2. Paint the cork with acrylic paint.
3. Put beads of various sizes and shapes on the wire. Don't place too many. They need room to move a little.
4. Glue a bead to the end of the wire.
5. Make a joyful sound by rubbing a dowel across the beads.

WOOSH / STICK

You will need:
- 2 cardboard tubes from paper towels (or 1 wrapping paper tube)
- 15 flathead nails, 1½" long
- duct tape
- decorative, self-adhesive paper
- assortment of rice, beans, popcorn kernels, and gravel

1. Tape paper towel tubes together to form one long tube, or use a wrapping paper tube.
2. Insert nails around the tube in a random pattern.
3. Trace the pattern for the tube ends onto cardboard. Cut them out. Secure one to the end of the tube with tape.
4. Use a funnel to pour in rice, beans, gravel, and popcorn. The total amount of the mixture should measure about ¾ cup.
5. Seal the open end of the tube. Cover the outside of the tube with decorative, self-adhesive plastic. Turn the woosh stick from end to end to hear a gentle wooshing sound.

Food–n–Fun

©1996 by the Standard Publishing Company. Permission is granted to reproduce this page for educational and ministry use only—not for resale.

FLOWER POT CHIMES

You will need:
- clay pots
- wood beads big enough to cover the holes in the bottom of the pots
- heavy, colorful cord

1. Begin from the bottom and work up. Tie a bead to the cord about a foot from the bottom, then thread the line up through the smallest clay pot.
2. Tie a bead 3-6" from the top of the pot and place another pot over the bead. Allow another 3-6", tie another bead, and top with the largest pot. Be sure each pot hangs about ⅓ of the way inside the one above it.
3. Tie a bead outside the top of the final pot. Tie the remaining cord into a loop.
4. Copy the eaglet onto a piece of wood. Paint as desired. Cut out the shape as shown. Punch a hole in the wood and attach to the bottom of the cord, as shown.

©1996 by the Standard Publishing Company. Permission is granted to reproduce this page for educational and ministry use only—not for resale.

Food-n-Fun

FUN WITH BUBBLES

FUNNEL

HANGER WIRE

Here are some fun things to use as bubble wands.

STRING

STRAW

STRAW

Put two straws together with string. Dip in bubble mix to get it wet. Pull tight and lift upward. Bring straws together to release bubble.

Lots of Bubble Mix
Mix ½ gallon water (bottled water works best), 1 cup of liquid soap, and 2 table-spoons of glycerin.

Bubble Art
Pour bubble mix into a baby food jar. Add 2 teaspoons food coloring. Blow bubbles onto white paper. As the bubbles hit the paper, they create a splattered design.

Put a person in a bubble?

Here's how: Put 2 gallons water (bottled water works best) into a wading pool. Add 2 cups liquid soap and 4 table-spoons glycerin. Mix carefully to avoid foam. Place a hoola-hoop into the pool and stand a person in the center of the hoop. Lift the hoop over the person.

Food–n–Fun

©1996 by the Standard Publishing Company. Permission is granted to reproduce this page for educational and ministry use only—not for resale.

REPRODUCIBLE PAGES

©1996 by the Standard Publishing Company. Permission is granted to reproduce this page for educational and ministry use only—not for resale.

Reproducibles

©1996 by the Standard Publishing Company. Permission is granted to reproduce this page for educational and ministry use only—not for resale.

Reproducibles

Reproducibles

©1996 by the Standard Publishing Company. Permission is granted to reproduce this page for educational and ministry use only—not for resale.

©1996 by the Standard Publishing Company. Permission is granted to reproduce this page for educational and ministry use only—not for resale.

Reproducibles

Ideas for using these letters:

★ Copy the alphabet and create some great posters and bulletin boards.

★ Copy the letters and play a game as you try to name objects that start with each letter.

★ Copy the letters and use them as the first initial on nametags.

★ Trace the letters with permanent markers on clear acetate (report covers work well) and decorate windows.

©1996 by the Standard Publishing Company. Permission is granted to reproduce this page for educational and ministry use only—not for resale.

Reproducibles

Attendance Chart—©1996 by the Standard Publishing Company. Permission is granted to reproduce this page for educational and ministry use only—not for resale.

Reproducibles

Peep Overs

To,

FROM!

Copy the Peep Overs, color them, and mount them on heavy cardboard. Cut them out and use them as decorations for cards or bookmarks. Enlarge the Peep Overs to use over the tops of doors. Give thanks to God for all His creation.

©1996 by the Standard Publishing Company. Permission is granted to reproduce this page for educational and ministry use only—not for resale.

Reproducibles

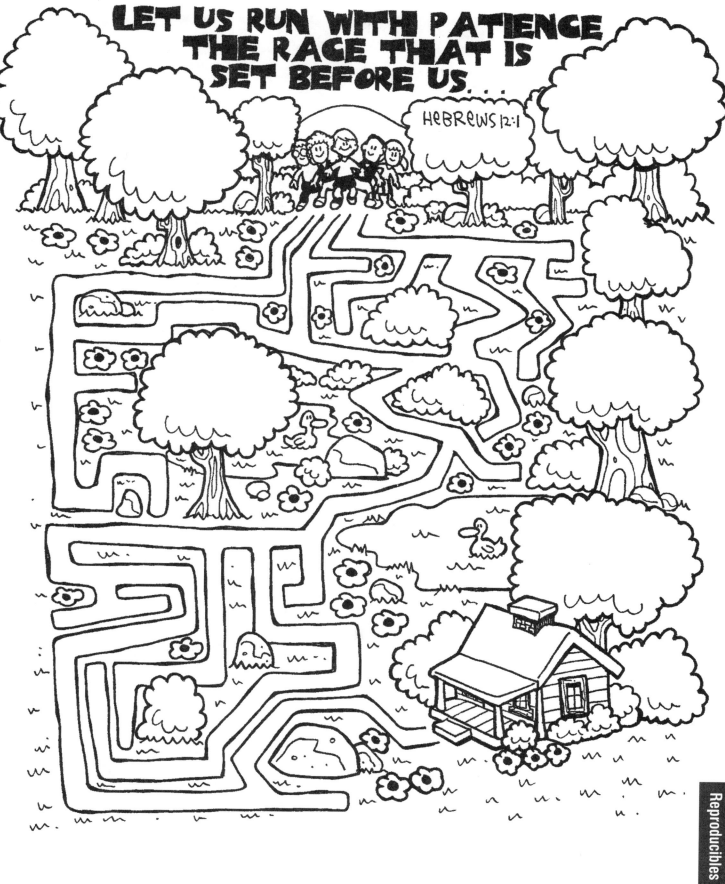

©1996 by the Standard Publishing Company. Permission is granted to reproduce this page for educational and ministry use only—not for resale.

©1996 by the Standard Publishing Company. Permission is granted to reproduce this page for educational and ministry use only—not for resale.

Reproducibles

©1994 Allison

©1996 by the Standard Publishing Company. Permission is granted to reproduce this page for educational and ministry use only—not for resale.

Reproducibles

BIBLE
BOOT
CANTEEN
ROPE
FLASHLIGHT
CRAYON
HOT DOG
CUPCAKE
WORM
CLOCK
WHISTLE
20 LADYBUGS

HIDDEN PICTURES

©1996 by the Standard Publishing Company. Permission is granted to reproduce this page for educational and ministry use only—not for resale.

Reproducibles

CERTIFICATE OF EXCELLENCE

©1994 Allison

PRESENTED TO

_____
NAME

FOR BEING A "CHAMP AT CAMP"

"BE OF GOOD COURAGE AND HE SHALL STRENGTHEN YOUR HEART. . ."

SIGNED _____
CAMP COACH

DATE _____

©1996 by the Standard Publishing Company. Permission is granted to reproduce this page for educational and ministry use only—not for resale.

Reproducibles

STAR PERSON AWARD GOES TO

NAME

SIGNED

DATE

YOU OUTSHINE THE STARS

©1996 by the Standard Publishing Company. Permission is granted to reproduce this page for educational and ministry use only—not for resale.

Reproducibles

NAME _____

WAS CAUGHT DOING A GREAT JOB

SIGNED _____   **DATE** _____

©1996 by the Standard Publishing Company. Permission is granted to reproduce this page for educational and ministry use only—not for resale.

Reproducibles

INDEX